GRAPHIC CARS

RACING CAR DRIVERS

by David West

illustrated by Peter Wilks *and* Geoff Ball

First published in 2010 by Franklin Watts

Franklin Watts
338 Euston Road
London NW1 3BH

Franklin Watts Australia
Level 17/207 Kent Street
Sydney, NSW 2000

A CIP catalogue record for this book is available from the British Library.

Dewey number: 796.7'2

ISBN: 978 0 7496 9251 3

Franklin Watts is a division of Hachette Children's Books, an Hachette UK company.
www.hachette.co.uk

GRAPHIC CAREERS: RACING CAR DRIVERS produced for Franklin Watts by
David West Children's Books, 7 Princeton Court,
55 Felsham Road, London SW15 1AZ

Copyright © 2008 David West Children's Books

Designed and produced by
David West Children's Books

Editor: Gail Bushnell

Photo credits:
5br, Rechlin; 6-7t, Dan Smith; 6-7m, Imperial Assassin; 6-7b, U.S. Air Force photo by
Larry McTighe; 7t, Rick Dikeman; 7m, Evil moe; 44-5, CIK/FIA Press releases GFDL.

Printed in China

Website disclaimer:
Note to parents and teachers: Every effort has been made by the Publishers to ensure
that the websites in this book are suitable for children, that they are of the highest
educational value, and that they contain no inappropriate or offensive material.
However, because of the nature of the Internet, it is impossible to guarantee that the
contents of these sites will not be altered. We strongly advise that Internet access is
supervised by a responsible adult.

CONTENTS

EARLY YEARS OF CAR RACING

On 19 December 1893, the French news magazine *Le Petit Journal* announced a trial for 'horseless carriages' from Paris to Rouen. A total of 21 vehicles took part in the event in 1894 and although it was not a race it ignited interest in automobiles.

Panhard-Levassor, 1895

Fernand Gabriel driving a Mors *in the Paris-Madrid 1903 race, which was stopped when eight people were killed and many more injured during the first day.*

THE FIRST RACE

After the success of the Paris-Rouen trial, it was thought that a race would be more exciting. Thus the first organised car race was held in 1895 on the open roads of France, from Paris to Bordeaux and back. Emile Levassor won the race in a *Panhard-Levassor* that had a top speed of 29.7 kilometres per hour.

BIGGER AND FASTER

These early racing events were both a proving ground for the new car makes and a shop window for people wanting to buy cars. Winning was all-important. Speeds increased as engine sizes grew. By 1908, massive engines of 12–13 litres, mounted on flimsy frames with only primitive brakes, propelled the cars up to 160 kilometres per hour.

A Bentley charges round the Le Mans 24-hour race circuit. The race tested a car's reliability as well as its speed.

INTERNATIONAL CAR RACING

Car racing became a major international sporting event when, in 1900, James Gordon Bennett, an American newspaper tycoon living in Paris, put up the cash and trophy for a series of races promoting a contest between national teams. However, there were many car manufacturers who could not enter due to the three-cars-per-team rule. Inevitably, other race events began

Start of the 1910 Vanderbilt Cup.

to appear. In 1904, William K. Vanderbilt organised a cup in his name in the United States and in 1906, the French held the first Grand Prix at Le Mans.

Indianapolis, 1912

THE PURE RACER

By the 1930s the high-priced road cars were transformed into pure racers, with Delage, Auto Union, Mercedes-Benz and Bugatti constructing streamlined cars with supercharged engines and extensive use of aluminium alloys. Apart from the Italian *Mille Miglia*, most races were now held on specially built tracks such as the Nurburgring in Germany and the Indianapolis Motor Speedway in the United States. By the 1950s, car racing events were held around the world, from single-seater (open wheel) to stock car racing, attracting huge crowds who craved the sights, sounds and smells of speed and danger.

Specially built race cars began to be made during the 1930s, like this Auto Union Type D.

TYPES OF AUTO RACING

Since 1895 car racing has become increasingly popular. As various regulations, formulas and racing organisations have formed over the years, so have the many variations of the sport.

CATEGORIES

One of the most popular forms of auto racing worldwide is single-seater (open wheel) racing. The best known is Formula One, which has an annual world championship for drivers and constructors. Touring car racing is popular in Europe and the US. It uses heavily modified street cars. The most popular form of auto sport in the US is NASCAR. The race cars look very like street cars, but underneath the lightweight bodies they are specialised racing machines. Another popular street-type car racing is rallying. The World Rally Championship is the top series, with events taking place all over the world. In sports car racing, specially built prototype cars and production sports cars compete on closed circuits. The most famous races are the 24 Hours of Le Mans and Daytona. One of the noisiest and fastest is drag racing, where two specialised vehicles compete along a 400 metre strip. These are just a few of the many types of auto racing. Others include Targa Racing (Targa Rally), one-make racing, production car racing, historical racing and hill climbing.

A Formula One Ferrari takes a bend at Indianapolis (above). GTP sports cars race at Lexington, Ohio (right).

Top methanol dragster at Santa Pod (left)

Henning Solberg drives a Peugeot 206 during the WRC Neste Rally, Finland (above).

NASCAR race cars hurtle around the Daytona 500 oval circuit (left).

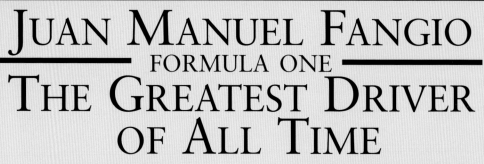

Juan Manuel Fangio
Formula One
The Greatest Driver of All Time

IT IS 1990. THE FAMOUS ARGENTINIAN RACING DRIVER FANGIO IS BEING INTERVIEWED ABOUT HIS RACE AT THE NURBURGRING, GERMANY, IN 1957.

THIS WAS THE BIG RACE OF THE YEAR. IF YOU WON THIS YOU WOULD WIN THE CHAMPIONSHIP FOR THE FIFTH TIME.

YES. I WAS STARTING IN POLE POSITION*. THE TWO BRITISH DRIVERS, MIKE HAWTHORN AND PETER COLLINS, WERE BEHIND ME IN THE FERRARIS.

MY MASERATI HAD PIRELLI TYRES, WHICH WERE GOOD FOR GRIP BUT WORE FASTER THAN THE HARDER ENGLEBERT TYRES THE FERRARIS WERE USING.

THEIR TYRES WOULD ALLOW THEM TO RACE WITHOUT STOPPING IN THE PITS, BUT I WOULD NEED TO CHANGE MY TYRES.

*FIRST POSITION ON THE START GRID.

'THE TWO FERRARIS SHOT OFF FIRST...'

AS THEY PASS THE FINISH LINE AFTER THE FIRST LAP, IT'S HAWTHORN, COLLINS AND FANGIO IN THIRD...

FANGIO HAD BETTER GET A MOVE ON, IF HE WANTS A 30-SECOND LEAD!

'I WAITED FOR AN OPENING TO GET BY...'

THESE GUYS ARE GOING LIKE FIREMEN!

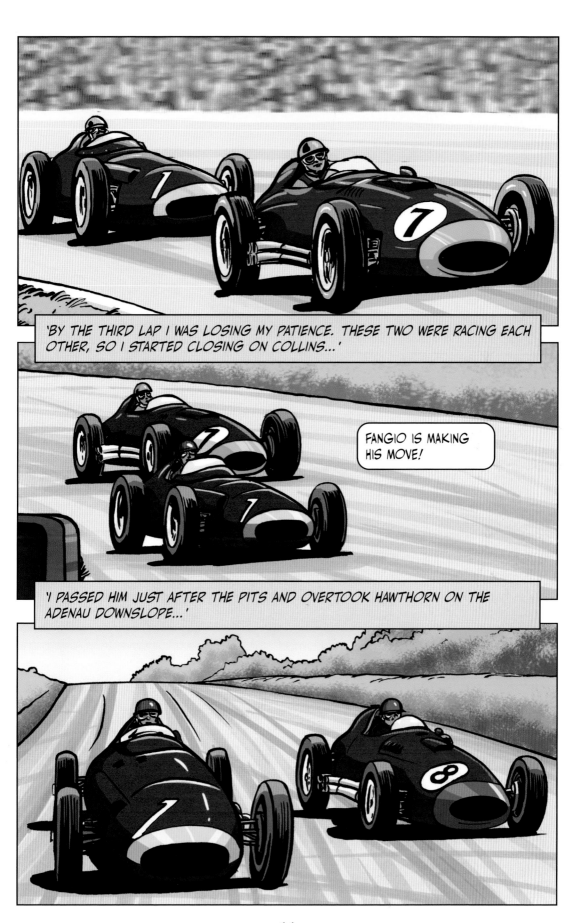

'BY THE THIRD LAP I WAS LOSING MY PATIENCE. THESE TWO WERE RACING EACH OTHER, SO I STARTED CLOSING ON COLLINS...'

FANGIO IS MAKING HIS MOVE!

'I PASSED HIM JUST AFTER THE PITS AND OVERTOOK HAWTHORN ON THE ADENAU DOWNSLOPE...'

'I WAS SO THIRSTY, I DRANK A WHOLE BOTTLE OF WATER. THE MECHANICS CHANGED THE TYRES AND REFUELLED THE CAR...'

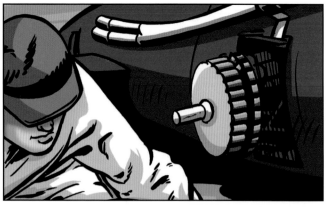

THE MECHANICS SHOULD HAVE FINISHED BY NOW.

'SUDDENLY I REALISED SOMETHING WAS WRONG...'

FANGIO IS STILL IN THE PITS AND THERE GO HAWTHORN AND COLLINS...

'THE MECHANICS HAD MESSED UP THE REFUELLING AND ONE OF THE WHEELS WOULDN'T COME OFF...'

'BY THE TIME I LEFT THE PITS I WAS 48 SECONDS BEHIND...'

WELL, THAT'S THE END OF A BEAUTIFUL DREAM.

'THE NEW TYRES TOOK A COUPLE OF LAPS TO WARM UP, WHICH MADE ME 51 SECONDS BEHIND...'

'AS THE TYRES BEDDED IN, I FOUND I WAS GAINING GROUND ON THE FERRARIS...'

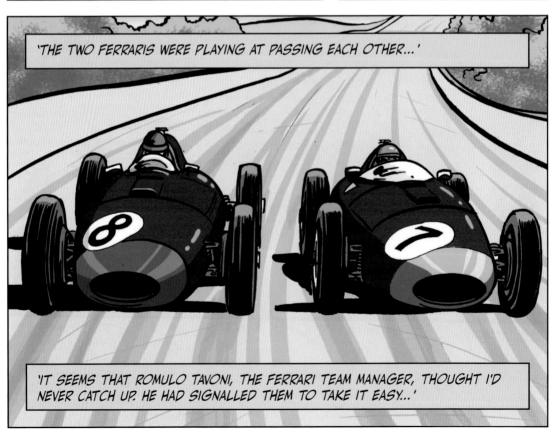

'THE TWO FERRARIS WERE PLAYING AT PASSING EACH OTHER...'

'IT SEEMS THAT ROMULO TAVONI, THE FERRARI TEAM MANAGER, THOUGHT I'D NEVER CATCH UP. HE HAD SIGNALLED THEM TO TAKE IT EASY...'

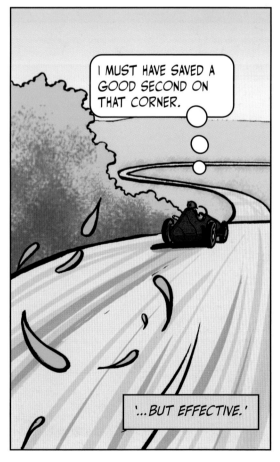

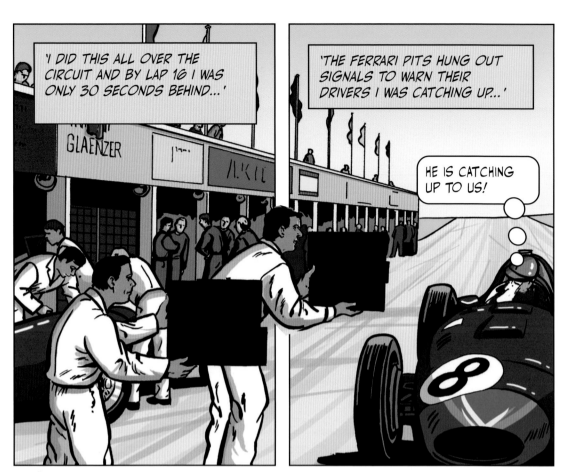

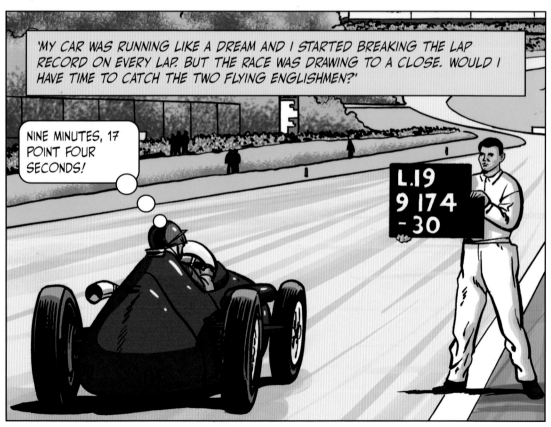

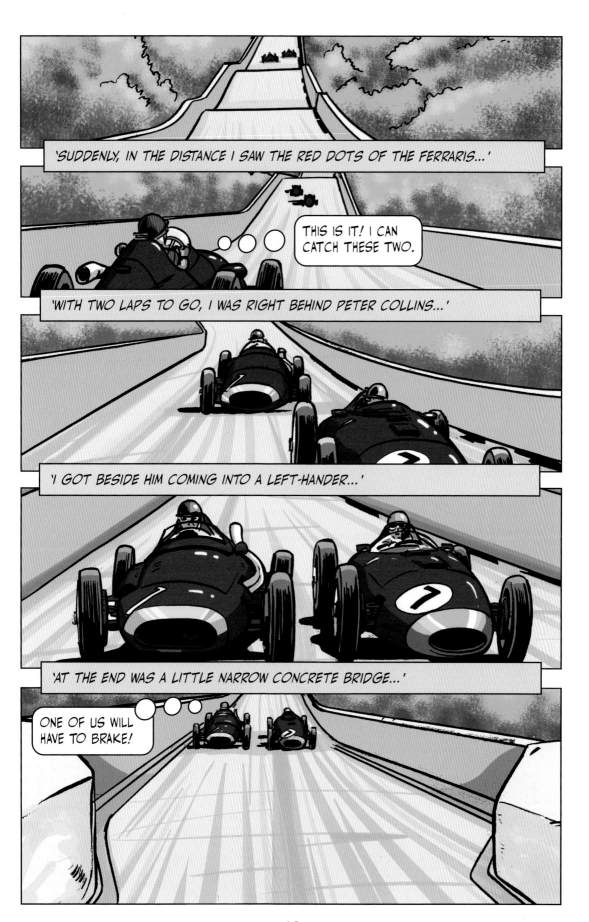

'AT THE LAST MOMENT, PETER BRAKED AND I WAS IN SECOND PLACE...'

'AND THERE WAS HAWTHORN, RIGHT IN FRONT OF ME. HE REALLY PILED IT ON...'

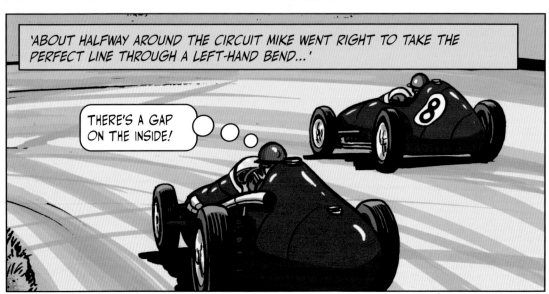

'ABOUT HALFWAY AROUND THE CIRCUIT MIKE WENT RIGHT TO TAKE THE PERFECT LINE THROUGH A LEFT-HAND BEND...'

THERE'S A GAP ON THE INSIDE!

FANGIO RETIRED FROM CAR RACING THE NEXT YEAR. HIS RECORD FIVE WORLD CHAMPIONSHIP TITLES STOOD FOR 45 YEARS. TODAY HE IS STILL CONSIDERED BY MANY TO BE THE GREATEST DRIVER OF ALL TIME.   *THE END*

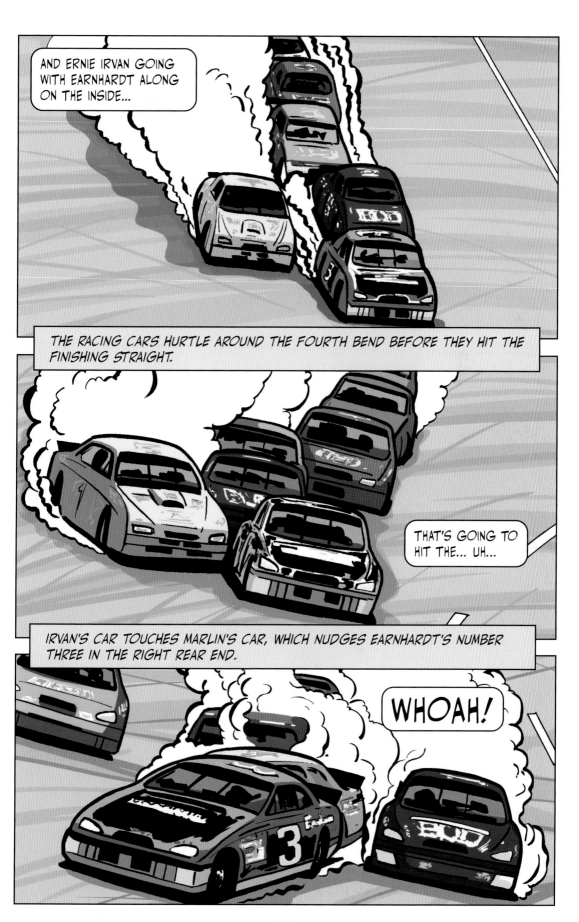

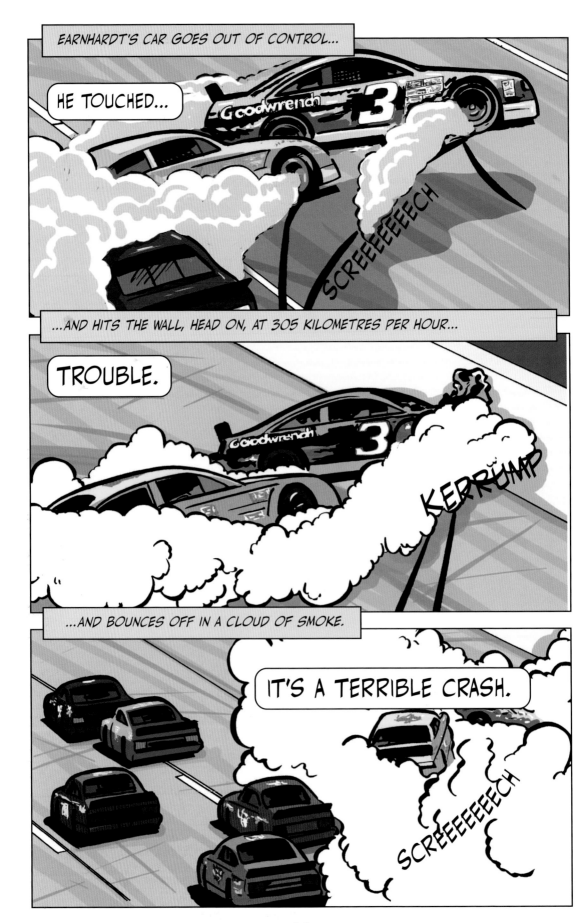

24

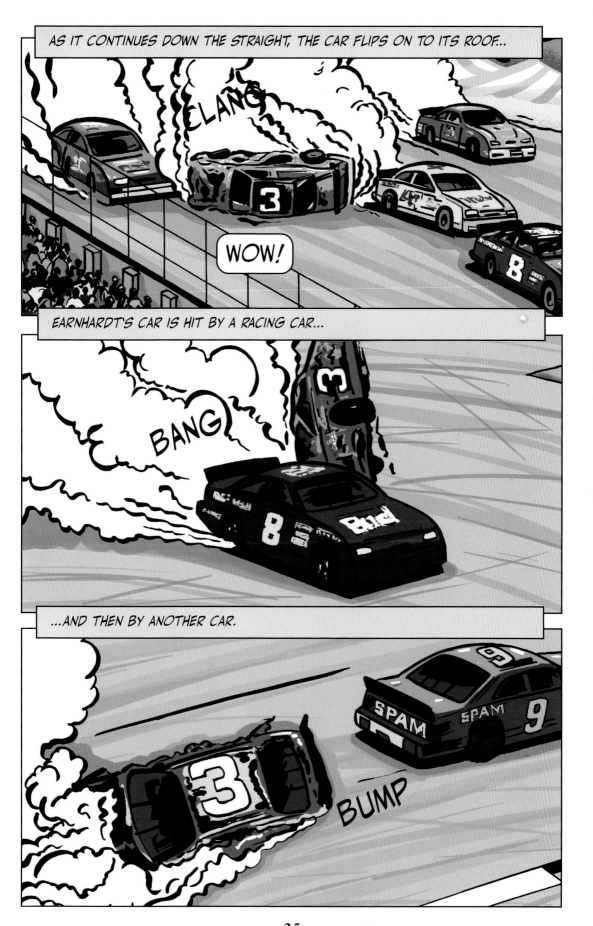

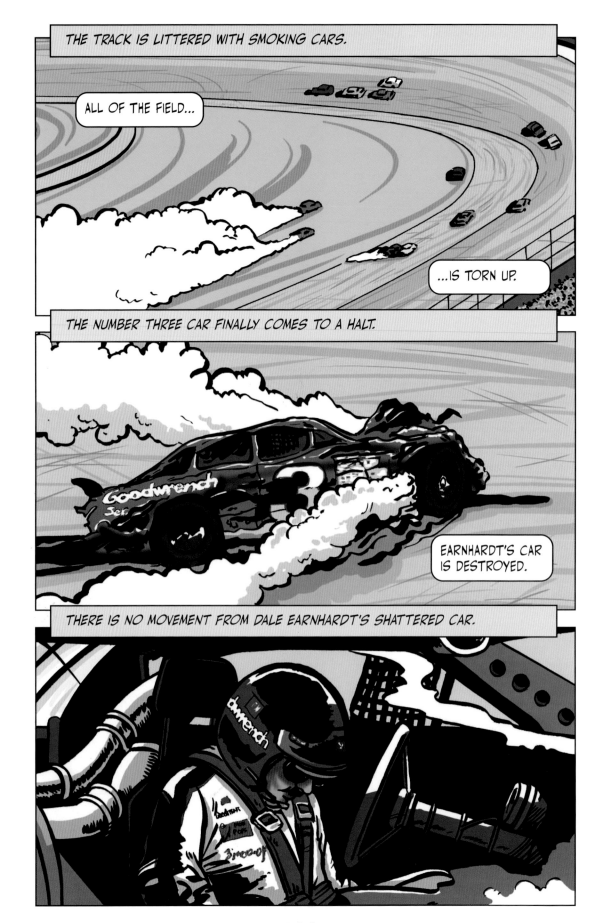

THE TRACK IS LITTERED WITH SMOKING CARS.

ALL OF THE FIELD...

...IS TORN UP.

THE NUMBER THREE CAR FINALLY COMES TO A HALT.

EARNHARDT'S CAR IS DESTROYED.

THERE IS NO MOVEMENT FROM DALE EARNHARDT'S SHATTERED CAR.

WITHIN SECONDS THE EMERGENCY VEHICLES ARRIVE AT EARNHARDT'S CAR.

EARNHARDT'S NUMBER THREE WENT HEAD ON INTO THE WALL AT 190 MILES PER HOUR!

IT LOOKS LIKE THEY'RE GOING TO HAVE TO CUT HIM OUT OF THE CAR.

THE HUSHED CROWD WAITS AS THE RESCUE CREWS WORK TO FREE THE DRIVER.

THEN, TO THE RELIEF OF THE CROWD...

EARNHARDT IS ON HIS FEET AND HE IS WALKING TO THE AMBULANCE.

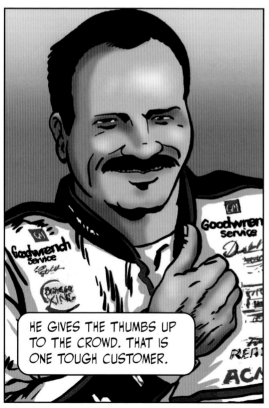

HE GIVES THE THUMBS UP TO THE CROWD. THAT IS ONE TOUGH CUSTOMER.

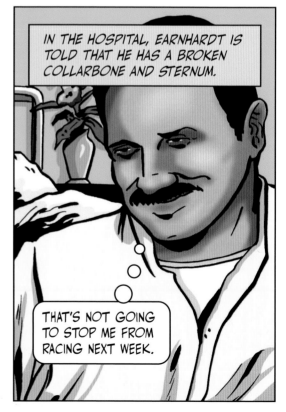

IN THE HOSPITAL, EARNHARDT IS TOLD THAT HE HAS A BROKEN COLLARBONE AND STERNUM.

THAT'S NOT GOING TO STOP ME FROM RACING NEXT WEEK.

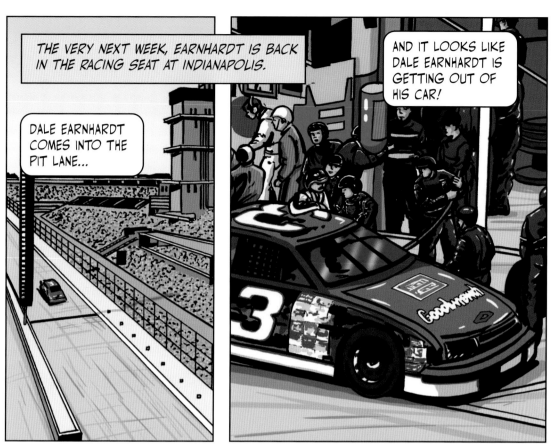

THE VERY NEXT WEEK, EARNHARDT IS BACK IN THE RACING SEAT AT INDIANAPOLIS.

DALE EARNHARDT COMES INTO THE PIT LANE...

AND IT LOOKS LIKE DALE EARNHARDT IS GETTING OUT OF HIS CAR!

LATER, AT AN INTERVIEW...

OBVIOUSLY THE INJURIES FROM LAST WEEK'S CRASH GOT TO YOU OUT THERE.

I TELL YOU, LEAVING THAT NUMBER THREE CAR WAS THE HARDEST THING I'VE EVER DONE.

BUT DALE EARNHARDT WAS NO QUITTER...

THE NEXT WEEKEND, DALE EARNHARDT CROSSES THE START/FINISH LINE DURING QUALIFICATION AT WATKINS GLEN, NEW YORK.

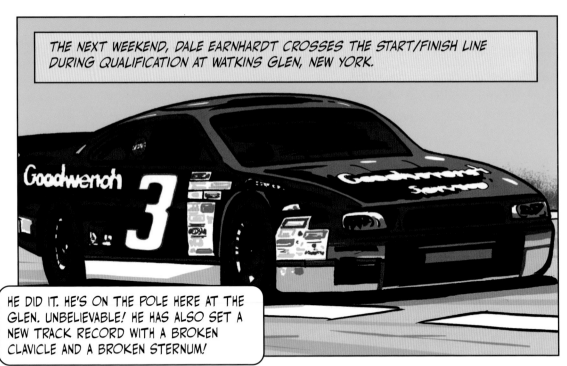

HE DID IT. HE'S ON THE POLE HERE AT THE GLEN. UNBELIEVABLE! HE HAS ALSO SET A NEW TRACK RECORD WITH A BROKEN CLAVICLE AND A BROKEN STERNUM!

ON RACE DAY, DALE EARHARDT FANS WEAR NEWLY PRINTED T-SHIRTS.

ON THE POLE AT THE GLEN
"It hurt so good!"

WHILE WAITING ON THE TRACK IN HIS CAR, EARNHARDT IS INTERVIEWED.

DALE, IS THIS THE DAY YOU STAY OR DO YOU COME OUT OF THE CAR?

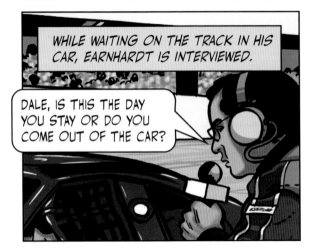

I'M A LITTLE SORE IN MY SHOULDER RIGHT NOW, BUT WE'LL JUST HAVE TO SEE HOW IT GOES.

EARNHARDT STARTS WELL AND LEADS THE RACE.

THIS GUY IS INCREDIBLE. TWO WEEKS AGO WE THOUGHT IT WAS ALL OVER FOR HIM...

EARNHARDT LEADS FOR MOST OF THE RACE, BUT THE PAIN WEARS HIM DOWN.

...AND EARNHARDT FINISHES SIXTH.

AT THE END OF THE SEASON, DALE EARNHARDT'S CHAMPIONSHIP POSITION WAS FOURTH. HE WAS NEVER TO ACHIEVE THAT EIGHTH CHAMPIONSHIP WIN. SADLY, HE WAS KILLED FIVE YEARS LATER, IN 2001, IN A CRASH AT THE DAYTONA 500.   THE END

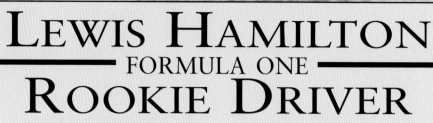

LEWIS HAMILTON
FORMULA ONE
ROOKIE DRIVER

IN 1992, A NEWS CREW FROM A CHILDREN'S TV SHOW IS FILMING A REMOTE-CONTROLLED RACING CAR EVENT.

THE WINNER IS A SEVEN-YEAR-OLD NAMED LEWIS HAMILTON.

IT IS THREE YEARS LATER. LEWIS HAS BEEN RACING KARTS, SMALL RACING CARS WITH NO SUSPENSION OR BODYWORK, IN THE SUPER ONE BRITISH CHAMPIONSHIP, FROM THE AGE OF EIGHT. HIS FATHER, ANTHONY, IS HIS MANAGER AND MECHANIC.

LEWIS WAITS WHILE HIS FATHER TINKERS WITH THE KART. HE REALLY WANTS TO WIN THE FINAL RACE.

IN THE LAST RACE, LEWIS IS CHEERED ON BY HIS FAMILY...

COME ON, LEWIS!

HE TAKES THE CHEQUERED FLAG IN FIRST PLACE.

LEWIS FINISHES THE SEASON BY WINNING THE SUPER ONE BRITISH CHAMPIONSHIP IN THE CADET CLASS.

THAT SAME YEAR, LEWIS IS AT THE AUTOSPORT AWARDS.

HE MEETS RON DENNIS, THE FORMULA ONE MCLAREN-MERCEDES TEAM BOSS.

I WANT TO RACE IN FORMULA ONE. CAN I DRIVE FOR YOUR TEAM?

FROM 1996 TO 1997, LEWIS CONTINUES TO RACE IN KARTS.

GO AND WIN SOME MORE RACES AND WE'LL SEE.

THE GOING IS TOUGH. HE HAS TO FIT SCHOOL IN BETWEEN THE BUSY RACE SCHEDULE AND TRAINING.

THERE IS LITTLE TIME TO SPEND WITH HIS FRIENDS. WHEN BULLIES TAKE AN INTEREST IN HIM...

NOBODY WILL BOTHER ME WHEN I BECOME A BLACK BELT.

...HE TAKES UP KARATE.

THE SPORT OF KARTING IS EXPENSIVE TO COMPETE IN. HIS FATHER HAS TO HOLD DOWN THREE JOBS.

WE NEED SOME SPONSORSHIP TO HELP PAY FOR ALL THIS.

BETWEEN 1996 AND 1997, LEWIS WINS FOUR MORE BRITISH KART TITLES.

THE FOLLOWING YEAR, RON DENNIS SIGNS LEWIS, AGED 13, FOR MCLAREN'S DEVELOPMENT PROGRAMME.

THERE IS NOW MONEY AND SUPPORT FOR LEWIS IN HIS RACING AND SCHOOLWORK.

WITH MCLAREN BEHIND HIM, LEWIS GOES ON TO WIN THE EUROPEAN KARTING CHAMPIONSHIP IN 2000, AT THE AGE OF 15. IN 2001 HE COMPETES IN THE SUPER-A WORLD KARTING CHAMPIONSHIP, FINISHING 15TH.

IN 2001, LEWIS MOVES INTO SINGLE-SEAT RACING CARS. THE FOLLOWING YEAR HE FINISHES THIRD IN THE FORMULA RENAULT CHAMPIONSHIP.

THIS IS MORE DIFFICULT THAN I FIRST THOUGHT IT WOULD BE!

AT THE NEXT ATTEMPT, HE WINS THE TITLE.

THIS IS MORE LIKE IT!

HE MOVES UP TO FORMULA THREE IN 2003. THE FIRST SEASON SEES HIM COMING IN FIFTH IN THE CHAMPIONSHIP. THE NEXT SEASON HE WINS 15 OUT OF THE 20 RACES AND WINS THE TITLE.

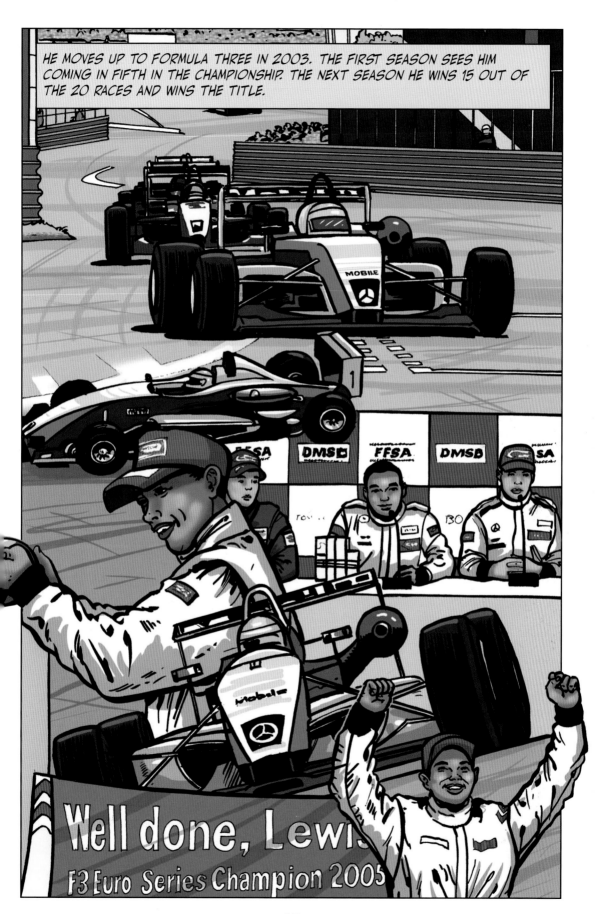

Well done, Lewis

F3 Euro Series Champion 2005

AFTER HIS SUCCESS IN FORMULA THREE, LEWIS IS SIGNED UP BY THE ART GRAND PRIX RACE TEAM FOR THE 2006 GP2 SERIES*.

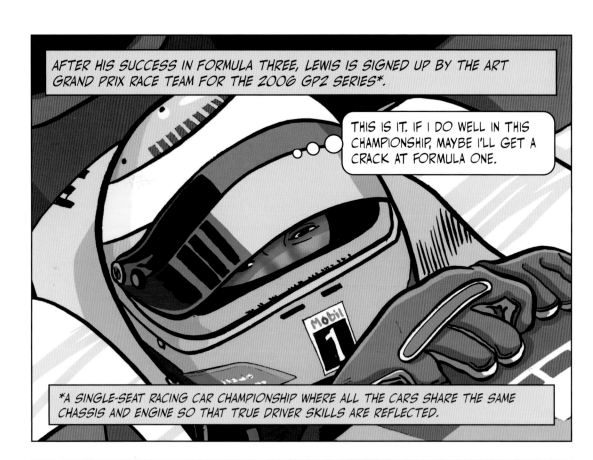

THIS IS IT. IF I DO WELL IN THIS CHAMPIONSHIP, MAYBE I'LL GET A CRACK AT FORMULA ONE.

*A SINGLE-SEAT RACING CAR CHAMPIONSHIP WHERE ALL THE CARS SHARE THE SAME CHASSIS AND ENGINE SO THAT TRUE DRIVER SKILLS ARE REFLECTED.

AT THE BRITISH GP2 RACE, AT SILVERSTONE, LEWIS'S SKILLS ARE IMPRESSIVE.

PIQUET AROUND THE OUTSIDE OF PICCHIONE...

AND HERE COMES HAMILTON. THEY ARE THREE WIDE INTO MAGGOTS.

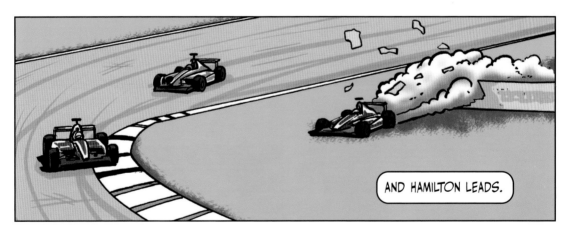

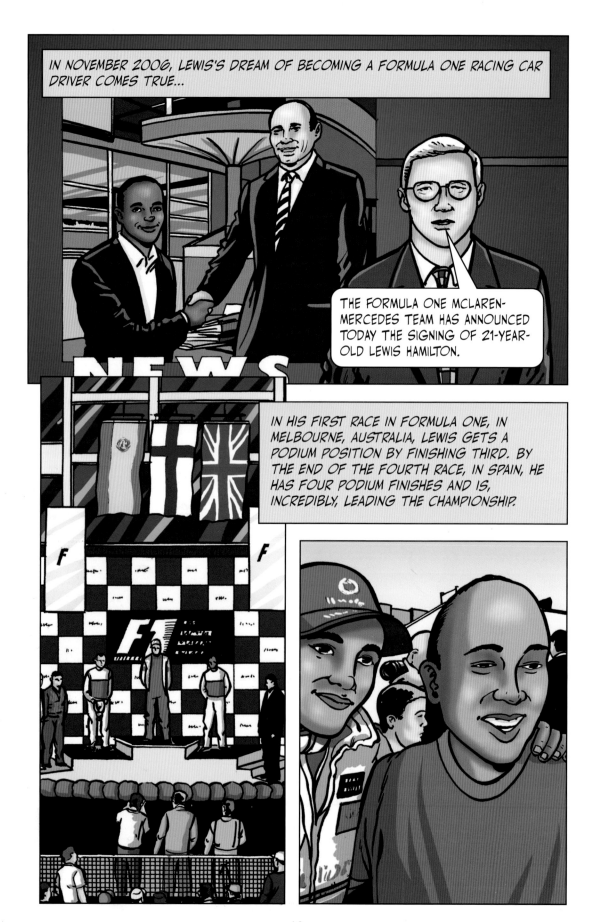

IN NOVEMBER 2006, LEWIS'S DREAM OF BECOMING A FORMULA ONE RACING CAR DRIVER COMES TRUE...

THE FORMULA ONE MCLAREN-MERCEDES TEAM HAS ANNOUNCED TODAY THE SIGNING OF 21-YEAR-OLD LEWIS HAMILTON.

IN HIS FIRST RACE IN FORMULA ONE, IN MELBOURNE, AUSTRALIA, LEWIS GETS A PODIUM POSITION BY FINISHING THIRD. BY THE END OF THE FOURTH RACE, IN SPAIN, HE HAS FOUR PODIUM FINISHES AND IS, INCREDIBLY, LEADING THE CHAMPIONSHIP.

AT THE BEGINNING OF THE SIXTH RACE, IN CANADA, LEWIS IS ON POLE POSITION FOR THE FIRST TIME.

HE BUILDS UP A 20-SECOND LEAD, BUT WHEN KUBICA CRASHES, THE SAFETY CAR COMES OUT AND THE REST OF THE CARS CATCH UP WITH HIM.

LEWIS STAYS COOL AND REMAINS IN FRONT. THE SAFETY CAR IS DEPLOYED A SECOND TIME AND AGAIN THE REST OF THE FIELD CATCHES UP...

'THE ROOKIE DRIVER, LEWIS HAMILTON, WINS HIS FIRST GRAND PRIX.'

BUT LEWIS IS TOO FAST FOR THE OTHERS AND GOES ON TO WIN HIS FIRST FORMULA ONE RACE. HE LEADS THE 2007 CHAMPIONSHIP UNTIL THE LAST RACE WHEN HIS CAR SUFFERS GEAR PROBLEMS AND HE MISSES WINNING IT BY ONE POINT. HE DOESN'T HAVE LONG TO WAIT. HE WINS THE CHAMPIONSHIP IN 2008.   **THE END**

HOW TO BECOME A RACING CAR DRIVER

The world of racing car driving is extremely competitive. Only the best will get to race cars.

FIRST THINGS FIRST

The first thing you should do is read as much as possible about the sport. Also, try to get to meet and talk with the people involved in the sport. From mechanics to drivers, they will all have valuable information to help you on your way to that ultimate goal. A good way to meet these people is to go to racetracks and if possible get a pit pass. Try volunteering for jobs such as selling tickets or ushering. After that try to get onto a race team. Offer to wash engines or polish the race car. Do whatever you can and talk to as many people as possible. The more time you spend around race circuits the more you will learn.

EARLY RACING

You can never be too young to start racing. Many of today's champions started racing karts at a very early age – Lewis Hamilton started racing at the age of eight. There are many local karting organisations, as well as the National Karting Association (NKA), which can supply information on training and race events. There are also racing schools, many of which can be found on the internet at www.rukmotorsport.com. Learning to race can be very expensive. Besides the cost of the racing machine, there are the costs of maintenance and transportation to the racing meetings. If drivers show promise, they may attract a sponsor who will carry part or all of the costs.

GLOSSARY

aggressive Pursuing something forcefully.

aluminium alloys Lightweight metals that are a mix of aluminium and another metal such as copper, zinc manganese, silicon or magnesium.

chassis A car's frame, on which the engine and other parts are fixed.

clavicle Collarbone.

formula The classification of a racing car, usually by engine size.

inevitable Certain to happen.

maintenance The process of keeping something in good condition.

modify To change something.

pits The part of a racetrack where the racing car is garaged and where teams can change tyres and refuel the car.

podium The raised platform where the winner, second-place and third-place drivers receive their trophies.

primitive Simple or basic.

promote To further the progress of something.

prototype The first working model of a machine (racing car).

regulations Rules made by an organisation.

sternum The breastbone.

streamlined Shaped to allow a car to have a small amount of air resistance.

supercharged Supplied with extra power, usually from a mechanical device attached to an engine, such as a turbocharger or supercharger.

tycoon A wealthy, powerful person in business or industry.

variation A difference or change from the norm.

volunteer A person who offers to work for an organisation, usually without pay.

FOR MORE INFORMATION

ORGANISATIONS

National Karting Association
Devonia, Long Road West
Dedham
Colchester C07 6ES
01206 322726
Email: enquiry@nationalkarting.co.uk
Website: http://www.nationalkarting.co.uk

Brooklands Museum
Brooklands Road
Weybridge
Surrey KT13 0QN
01932 857381
Email: info@brooklandsmuseum.com
Website: http://www.brooklandsmuseum.com

FOR FURTHER READING

Gifford, Clive. *Formula 1* (Motorsports). London, England: Franklin Watts, 2009.

Gilpin, Daniel & Pang, Alex. *Record Breakers* (Machines Close-Up). London, England: Wayland, 2009.

Hammond, Richard. *Car Science*. London, England: Dorling Kindersley, 2008

Kelley, K. C. *NASCAR Racing to the Finish*. London, England: Reader's Digest, 2005.

Wilson, Hugo. *Renault Formula One Motor Racing Book*. London, England: Dorling Kindersley, 2006.

INDEX

Keeping Unusual Pets

RATS

June McNicholas

www.heinemann.co.uk/library
Visit our website to find out more information about Heinemann Library books.

To order:
☎ Phone 44 (0) 1865 888066
🖹 Send a fax to 44 (0) 1865 314091
🖥 Visit the Heinemann Bookshop at www.heinemann.co.uk/library to browse our catalogue and order online.

First published in Great Britain by Heinemann Library, Halley Court, Jordan Hill, Oxford OX2 8EJ
a division of Reed Educational and Professional Publishing Ltd. Heinemann is a registered trademark
of Reed Educational and Professional Publishing Ltd.

OXFORD MELBOURNE AUCKLAND JOHANNESBURG BLANTYRE
GABORONE IBADAN PORTSMOUTH (NH) USA CHICAGO

© Reed Educational and Professional Publishing Ltd 2002
First published in paperback 2003
The moral right of the proprietor has been asserted.

Designed by Celia Floyd
Originated by Dot Gradations Limited
Printed in Hong Kong/China by Wing King Tong

ISBN 0 431 12402 7 (hardback)
06 05 04 03 02
10 9 8 7 6 5 4 3 2 1

ISBN 0 431 12405 1 (paperback)
07 06 05 04 03
10 9 8 7 6 5 4 3 2 1

British Library Cataloguing in Publication Data

McNicholas, June
  Rats. – (Keeping unusual pets)
  1. Rats as pets – Juvenile literature
  I. Title
  636.9'352

Acknowledgements
The Publishers would like to thank the following for permission to reproduce photographs: Ardea/Johan De
Meester: p. 20 (bottom); Bruce Coleman Collection/Andrew Purcell: p. 42; Bruce Coleman Collection/Jane
Burton: p. 7 (top); Gareth Boden: pp. 5 (top), 5 (bottom), 8 (top), 8 (bottom), 9 (top), 9 (bottom), 11 (top),
11 (bottom), 12, 14, 15, 18 (top), 18 (bottom), 19 (top), 19 (bottom), 20 (top), 21, 22, 23 (top), 23 (bottom), 24,
25 (top), 25 (bottom), 26 (top), 26 (bottom), 27, 28, 29 (left), 29 (right), 31 (top), 31 (bottom), 33 (top),
33 (bottom), 35 (top), 35 (bottom), 37 (top), 40, 44 (top), 44 (bottom); Maria Joannou: p. 43; NHPA/Daniel
Heuclin: p. 39; NHPA/Stephen Dalton: p. 7 (bottom); Science Photo Library: pp. 4, 10, 13; Tudor Photography:
pp. 6, 16, 17 (top), 17 (bottom), 30, 32 (top), 32 (bottom), 34, 36, 37 (bottom), 38, 41, 45 (top), 45 (bottom).

Thanks also to Kathy Gowenlock and family, and the staff of 'Happy Pets' in Droitwich Spa.

Cover photograph reproduced with permission of NHPA/Daniel Heuclin.

Every effort has been made to contact copyright holders of any material reproduced in this book.
Any omissions will be rectified in subsequent printings if notice is given to the Publishers.

Disclaimer
All the Internet addresses (URLs) given in this book were valid at the time of going to press. However, due to
the dynamic nature of the Internet, some addresses may have changed, or sites may have changed or ceased
to exist since publication. While the author and Publishers regret any inconvenience this may cause readers,
no responsibility for any such changes can be accepted by either the author or the Publishers.

No animals were harmed during the process of taking photographs for this series.